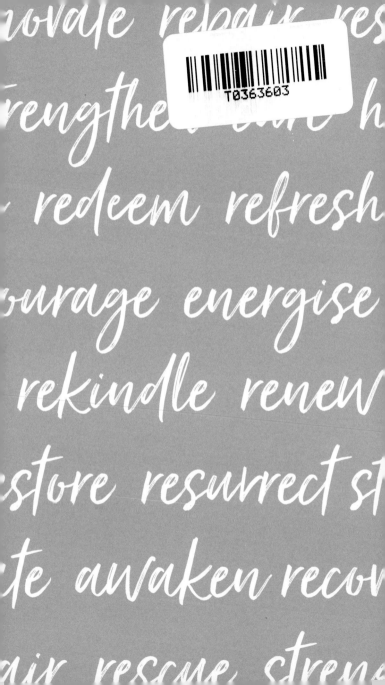

RESTORE

THE ESSENTIALISTS

MICHAEL JOSEPH
an imprint of
PENGUIN BOOKS

The only way to find true happiness and a sense of belonging is by restoring self-love, giving back and nourishing the whole of you: mind, body and soul.

DEBORAH HUTTON

To me, 'restore' means doing whatever you need to do for your mind and body to truly allow yourself to live your dream life every day – a life designed by you, for you.

KRISTINA KARLSSON – KIKKI.K FOUNDER

It's so important to give back to ourselves. For me, the daily yogic practices allow me to realign my mind and body.

DUSTIN BROWN – YOGI

'Restore' means renewal of your vital energy flow – the current within that directs you to greater fulfilment, happiness and purpose in life.

SHIV JYOTI – SPIRITUAL MENTOR

We often feel that we are too tired to move but our bodies NEED to move. When you discover that moving your body gives you more energy, that is when you truly break through.

SAM WOOD – FOUNDER OF 28

What I find most restorative is remaining directly engaged and connected to community.

KYLIE KWONG – CHEF

Sometimes we just need to stop. Finding my new purpose or drive is what fuels me, to make a difference and create change.

MARYANNE SHEARER — T2 CO-FOUNDER

'Restoring' is my self-love, self-care superpower.

DR JAMES ROUSE — NATUROPATH

You can't update software with open applications. You must close them. You must stop and unplug so that your system can restore.

LYDIA LASSILA — OLYMPIC CHAMPION

Travel is my great restorer – it fills the spirit, expands the mind, and fuels creativity.

CHRISTINE MANFIELD — CHEF

To restore my mind, body and spirit. I rely on self-care rituals that fill up my cup.

MEREDITH GASTON — ARTIST

When we are running on empty, our body does its best to let us know that it is time to slow down, rest, repair and restore. Too many people ignore this, swallow another pill, or write it off to getting old.

DR LIBBY WEAVER PHD — NUTRITIONAL BIOCHEMIST & SPEAKER

Contents

While the utmost care has been taken in researching and compiling RESTORE, the information contained in this book is not intended as a substitute for professional medical advice. Unless otherwise stated, alternative therapies are not evidence-based and are not proven to provide any medical benefit. You should always obtain professional advice from a medical practictioner before making lifestyle changes relating to your health.

MICHAEL JOSEPH

UK | USA | Canada | Ireland | Australia
India | New Zealand | South Africa | China

Penguin
Random House
Australia

First published by Penguin Random House Australia Pty Ltd, 2019

Text copyright © Shannah Kennedy and Lyndall Mitchell 2019

The moral right of the authors has been asserted.

Addresses for the Penguin Random House group of companies can be found at global.penguinrandomhouse.com/offices.

Cover design, internal floral illustrations and text design by Louisa Maggio © Penguin Random House Australia Pty Ltd
Cover branch vector by kosmofish/Shutterstock
Author photograph by Susan Bradfield
Typeset in Harriet by Louisa Maggio
Printed and bound in Hong Kong

A catalogue record for this book is available from the National Library of Australia

NATIONAL LIBRARY OF AUSTRALIA

ISBN 978 0 14379 631 2

penguin.com.au

To our children, Jack, Mia, Poppy and Grace.

We hope we have inspired you to be brave, unique,
adventurous, loving, kind, compassionate and bold.
We encourage you to never lose sight of the importance
of looking after yourself, nourishing your soul and
guarding your energy. You are more than beauty. You
are an amazing, complex mixture of emotion, wonder,
energy and personality. Don't ever limit yourself and
may you always have these precious attributes.

To our husbands.

Thank you for always supporting us with time,
space and respect so we can follow our passion and
live life authentically.

To those who want to learn.

May this be your retreat.

INTRODUCTION

Restore is a guide that you can dip into in order to nurture, nourish, reconnect and refuel. It is a collection of simple disciplines of life-transforming habits, and is designed to inspire you to re-centre and honour yourself. The *Restore* principles contribute to your wellbeing throughout your entire lifetime as they are essential elements for you to implement and master along your personal journey. They are an incredibly powerful reflection of your level of health, happiness and fulfilment.

We want to share with you these essential elements that we use in our lives. They are the practices at the forefront of our minds, and many are vital. The life and wellness skills in this book come from our combined 30 years of learning, and from insights gained by coaching and mentoring people from all walks of life.

These tools are used in our busy lives and keep us fulfilled, energetic and inspired each day. They are nourishing habits that will help you to reclaim your vitality and zest for life. They will nurture your soul, soak into your character and reward you with incredible self-confidence. We have seen these skills transform lives. We see our clients truly connect with themselves and live life with purpose using these self-care practices. It is a beautiful thing to watch.

Restore is a catalyst for creating positive changes in simple, sustainable ways. The book is empowering and educational, full of questions and insights, to allow your life to flow smoothly. This is our gift to you. Slow down, tune in, rebalance, restore.

Shannah and Lyndall – The Essentialists

1

MASTER
THE
PAUSE

Hold us in silence.
Do not throw
us back into
some discussion.

———

RUMI

When we pause, we give ourselves time to think and space to breathe, so we can make the best decisions. Each time we pause, we take small steps towards rebalancing and reconnecting with who we really are, our dreams and deepest desires. Each pause is a moment that we give ourselves to gently unwind. Learning to switch off and press the pause button in life is vital. It's like taking a big, soul-nourishing breath to find clarity, energy and space. Finding solitude and silence gives us the ability to shape and adjust our lives. It can reconnect us to our authentic self, highlight our inner strength and enable us to satisfy our own needs and desires, rather than relying on others.

Solitude gives us the space to think, dream, nourish and restore ourselves. So often we overschedule our days and nights and get stuck on a treadmill, pleasing others before ourselves. We push through, too tired to keep running and too scared to stop. Solitude is about creating some breathing space in the long race of life, and allowing room to let life flow. It eases the feeling of suffocation and allows space for clarity to come. The busier you are, the more important it is to take time out regularly in order to keep your body, mind and soul restored and in their most powerful state.

Solitude can feel uncomfortable at first; however, creating regular quiet time could be the key to becoming the best version of you and living with clarity and energy. When you pause to take care of yourself, you become the person you were always meant to be. You reclaim the right to live a momentous life.

Below you will find just some of the high-impact benefits you'll gain with every moment of 'alone time' you allocate for yourself. You will find it:

1. **INCREASES SELF-CONNECTION** – When you listen to your body and mind, you are more likely to make decisions that align with your values and your own personal capacity. You will feel happier and calmer.

2. **BRINGS YOUR VISION TO LIFE** – By creating the space, you can regularly revisit and reconfirm your goals and your vision. This helps you to stay on track and not start living someone else's dream.

3. **BUILDS POWERFUL MENTAL RESILIENCE** – By taking time in silence, you can calm your mind and meditate. This mental training helps to build your resilience and strengthen your mind.

4. **BOOSTS CREATIVITY** – Our creativity comes out when we allow space. We need peace and quiet to work out solutions, to have those 'aha' moments, and to create our own ways to do tasks.

5. **REDUCES STRESS** – Taking time to be alone for a few moments (maybe in the middle of the park on a sunny day) can be immensely helpful when you're trying to regain your mental centre.

6. **INCREASES PRODUCTIVITY** – Reclaiming your power of concentration and taking the time you need to complete projects can be very beneficial. At work, look for breakout rooms, mute any devices that might distract you, and work on projects in a scheduled way so that you can maximise your productivity.

7. **ENHANCES RELATIONSHIPS** – Solitude enriches our relationships with others. When we step back, it enables us to gain perspective and to be empathetic, rather than reacting to things in the moment.

PREPARING FOR SILENCE AND SOLITUDE

Here are a few things to consider before you give silence and solitude a try:

DECIDE ON A TIME FRAME – The exact length of time you need really depends on your own situation, but it's important to organise a dedicated period rather than just leaving it to fate.

CHOOSE YOUR LOCATION – To help minimise everyday distractions, it is really useful to get away from your usual living environment. You could go on a retreat or simply go for a walk or to a café.

EXPLAIN YOUR INTENTIONS to the people closest to you. Others will respect you for carving out this time for yourself, whether it is half an hour a day, a day a month or a part of your weekly routine.

HOW TO SPEND YOUR TIME IN SILENCE AND SOLITUDE

There are a few activities you can try during your time in solitude that will help to improve your self-knowledge. Remember to set an intention of what you want to achieve during this time. Is it to sit still and reflect? Or to write, listen or move slowly to the beat of your own drum?

MEDITATE – With regular meditation comes the ability to bring insight into our lives.

THINK – Periods of silence and solitude lend themselves well to strategic thinking and planning. Clarity is often the incredible result.

CREATE – Having the space to brainstorm ideas can be the starting point to unleashing your creativity. Be bold with your thoughts; there's no one else around to dismiss them.

RECONNECT – Use your alone time to really study the world around you. Touch the grass, smell the flowers, watch the clouds, be in nature. You will restore your sense of place in the world.

The best teacher is not in the mountains, or a hut, or an ice cave in the Himalayas, it is already within us. Giving yourself permission to press the pause button allows you to replenish your energy levels, process your thoughts and consider the world you have created for yourself. Sit with it and understand it. As the noise within starts to quieten, the world around you reflects this. Life becomes less of a struggle, and everything begins to flow. It is in this incredible space that we can make well-informed, clear and powerful decisions to return us to our natural state of balance.

2

REPRIORITISE
REST

Sleep
is the best
meditation.

———

DALAI LAMA

Sleep is how the body restores its power. It is the most essential and critical daily habit to master in order to flourish in life and enjoy this one precious journey.

Think about how you feel after a great night's sleep. How your outlook on life is more positively charged, and how much easier it is to exercise, make great food choices, be tolerant, patient and creative. Often in our work we see clients shaving time off this most important resource in an effort to get more done. As life gets busier, the art of sleep and restoration takes a back seat. Many people think their sleep deprivation is a badge of honour, but it's actually an act of self-sabotage, depletes our cells, muscles and organs, and can contribute to a more negative frame of mind.

If you want to be productive, healthy, vibrant and open to life's great experiences, sleep is essential. It's a fundamental part of your health and wellness. Sleep can make the difference between a successful, happy, productive life and a colourless, plodding existence. It is in your control and can take you from surviving to thriving.

To maintain optimum health, adults need between seven and eight hours of sleep per night. It is the amount of time our minds and bodies need to replenish, refuel and restore. Getting fewer than seven hours a night robs our health reserves and can lead to a worn-out immune system, lack of concentration, increased forgetfulness, poor decision-making and irritability. We lose our vibrancy and confidence.

It's thought that people who get fewer than seven hours of sleep are nearly three times as likely to develop a cold compared to those who get at least eight hours. Therefore, getting that extra hour could be the difference between you picking up a cold and staying healthy.

There are so many reasons why sleep is a core part of our mental health and wellbeing. Firstly, it acts like a dishwasher for our brain. During the day our brain collects harmful waste proteins. These proteins are washed away by sleep, which prepares our minds and bodies for the next day. Secondly, it takes time to process everything we have learned and experienced during the day. While we sleep, our brains are busy encoding all the new information we have absorbed throughout the day.

There are some factors that influence both the quality and quantity of your sleep. Here are some soothing sleep rituals to nurture yourself and have you snoring in no time.

1. **CONSISTENT BEDTIMES** – The most restorative time for your body to sleep is between 10 pm and 2 am. Get to bed by 10 pm whenever possible to honour your body and mind.

2. **TECHNOLOGY-FREE ZONES** – Remove any electronic devices from the bedroom and buy an old-fashioned alarm clock. Some experts believe that blue light from devices has a negative effect on the body. This light interrupts the body's production of melatonin, a fundamental chemical needed for sleep.

3. **TECHNOLOGY CURFEWS** – Turn off televisions, laptops and mobile devices one hour before bed (ideally by 9 pm) to allow your mind the time it needs to unwind before bed.

4. **THE SLUMBER ENVIRONMENT** – Strive to make your sleeping area an oasis, with limited light, little to no noise, and a nice cool temperature.

We create intentional sleep environments for babies with night lights and lullaby music, so why don't we do this for ourselves? The same principles still apply for adults, and yet we try to complicate things. Our bodies thrive with a great sleep routine. Intentionally create an environment for unwinding. Light a candle; be mindful of the types of television show you are watching right before bed; have some relaxing herbal tea to calm the nervous system; do some stretches; write in a journal; use an essential oil on your temples to calm the mind.

5. **FOOD AND DRINK** – Pay close attention to what you eat and drink in the evenings. Heavy dinners, caffeine and alcohol can make it difficult to fall and stay asleep.

6. **CONSISTENT RISING TIMES** – Get up at the same time every day to make it easier for your body's natural alarm clock. On the weekends when you need to top up your sleep tank, take a guilt-free siesta. This is the most effective way to keep your body in a rhythm for your weekly routine, but it's not for everyone. For some of us it may impact negatively on our evening sleep. So, listen to your body and choose what is right for you.

7. **PILLOW HEAVEN** – Buy a pillow that you love and that your head can sink into. Give your body the comfort it craves.

8. **DARKER AND COOLER** – A dark and cool room helps the quality of your sleep as your body works in rhythm with the natural light and air.

9. **ATTITUDE OF GRATITUDE** – An attitude of gratitude makes you more aware of the good things in your life. This positive outlook helps keep pessimism and worry at bay. It's no surprise that a number of studies have linked gratitude to greater happiness, satisfaction with life and optimism about the future. May your last thoughts be those of gratitude before you close down for the day.

10. **ESSENTIAL OILS** – Choose a relaxing, sleep-inducing essential oil and massage a few drops onto a specific part of your body, such as your forehead, neck, chest, wrists, hands or toes. Lavender is the perfect oil to start with as it helps calm the mind and reduce anxiety.

Sleep truly is your daily reset button. No matter what has happened during the day, sleep gives you the opportunity to reset and have more energy and perspective the next day. Sleep is not the luxury we often make it out to be. Good sleep is a necessity, non-negotiable, and it is the essential link and contributor to our overall health.

3

RENEW AND
REFUEL

Healing is every breath.

———

THICH NHAT HANH

Breathing. We do it every day. We don't even need to think about it. But what if we actually did take the time to think about it? Not just regular shallow breathing, but rather the deep, saturating breaths that make our skin tingle. It's a powerful tool and vital practice for influencing individual health and wellbeing, and the best part is that all the ingredients are free and right under our noses.

Breathing is fundamental for life. It provides our body with the oxygen it needs to create energy within our cells and expel waste products. It is vital to our very being and it is our life force. Without breath, we cease to exist.

When we watch a child breathe, we see the uninterrupted pure form of breath, the way nature intended. The belly rises on the inhalation and falls on the exhalation. This is also called belly breathing, diaphragmatic breathing or abdominal breathing. The restorative rhythm of breathing helps balance out our sympathetic and parasympathetic nervous systems, allowing our bodies to function more optimally.

In everyday life, the full, deep breath is what keeps our energy high, our minds focused and clear, and our nervous system calm and confident. Every deep breath we take helps to reverse lethargy and tiredness.

Once we start breathing deeply, our lungs will crave the oxygen boost and that becomes our new set point.

When we find ourselves feeling stressed and anxious, we start to chest-breathe, which only uses approximately 50 per cent of our lung capacity. This habit of shallow breathing starves our nervous system and triggers a fight or flight response whereby we feel threatened. When our body thinks we are in danger, it is not important to breathe deeply as we need to consume maximum amounts of oxygen as quickly as possible. This is our reserve response for emergencies. We are triggering our fight or flight stress response many times a day by breathing too shallowly, and this has a huge toll on our health and can cause premature ageing.

More importantly, controlled deep breathing can be used as a method to train the body's reaction to stressful situations and reduce or reverse the production of harmful stress hormones.

By learning how to breathe well we will become healthier and stronger. It also helps us to control our emotions, whether that be anger, frustration or fear, and keep a clear and sharp mind. Breathing is what recharges our cells, muscles and organs. Just like putting a phone on charge, we can go from the red zone to the green zone quickly. It connects our thoughts and feelings to our instincts and values; it is the connector between mind and body.

For a long time, deep, controlled breathing has been a key element of meditation, yoga, tai chi and qi gong; however, breath work is now becoming a discipline in its own right, with deep-breathing classes, one-on-one sessions and apps dedicated to the practice. For years the focus has predominantly been on the mental and psychological benefits of breath work, but fitness industry professionals are increasingly saying that it can also enhance athletic performance or speed up muscle recovery after a workout.

Because breathing is so basic and automatic, it is easy to ignore. So the next time someone tells you to take a deep breath, smile and heed their wise advice.

Here are some benefits of deep breathing:

- **Controlling your breathing** calms your brain and helps to reduce anxiety, depression and stress.
- **Counting breaths** taps into the brain's emotional control regions, helping to regulate our emotions and develop emotional intelligence.
- **Controlled breathing** may help boost the immune system and improve the metabolism, increasing energy levels and vitality.
- **Deep breathing** can relax your nervous system, lower your blood pressure and ease tense muscles.

The best part of using your breath as a tool to enhance your health and wellbeing is that there is no equipment needed and you can do it any time. To create the habit of breathing deeply, we suggest linking it to an activity that you already do so it becomes an automated habit. Some ways to make a start:

- **Take three deep breaths** before you get out of bed.
- **Take three deep breaths** when you turn the shower on.
- **Take three deep breaths** before every meal.
- **Take three deep breaths** when you start your computer every day.
- **Take three deep breaths** before you go to sleep at night.

What may seem like an insignificant start will add up over time to become a habit that supports your energy and vitality. What you do every day matters, and the habit of breathing deeply is no exception. Making sure you take those three deep breaths each day is better than a full day of shallow chest breathing.

DEEP-BREATHING TECHNIQUE

BELLY BREATHING

The first technique you need to learn is called 'belly breathing'. This is the most basic and most important of the breathing methods and you should master it before trying out the other techniques. It's very simple and requires just a few steps.

First, sit comfortably or lie down, depending on personal preference. Place your left hand on your stomach, just below your ribcage. Place your right on the centre of your chest.

Deepen the breath by breathing in through your nostrils for a count of four and breathing out for a count of four. Let your left hand rise and fall with your stomach. Slowly repeat three to ten times.

By learning how to deep-breathe properly, you will help to lower stress levels and ward off adrenal fatigue. Most breathing methods can be practised at home or in the office and take only a few minutes each day. Since breathing is something we can control and regulate, it is an effective tool for achieving a relaxed and clear state of mind. A regular practice of deep breathing is one of the best tools for improving your health and wellbeing.

Performing the belly-breathing technique twice daily for three to five minutes can produce long-term benefits. You can also use this technique any time you are feeling stressed or notice that your breathing has become constricted. By training your body with a regular practice of deep-breathing, you will begin to breathe more effectively even without concentrating on it. Your breath is your personal resource, an anchor point to always come back to. It connects you with the world around you.

4

REKINDLE
SELF-CARE

Put yourself at the top of your to-do list every single day and the rest will fall into place.

———

UNKNOWN

Self-care is about the most precious person in your life – YOU! Self-love grows from actions that support your physical, mental, emotional and spiritual growth. It is an intentional action, not just a state of feeling good. Self-love is dynamic: when we act in ways that expand self-love in us, we begin to accept our weaknesses as well as our strengths. We start to develop more compassion for ourselves as human beings.

Self-love is movement against mediocrity. It is being able to put yourself first and having a deep level of care for your own happiness. It is honouring the opportunity of life that you have been given and developing who you are. It is about giving yourself permission to make yourself a priority. The easiest way to increase your self-love is by practising self-care. The act of self-care is a concept that sounds easy in theory but often isn't as straightforward in practice. Self-care is what restores us, nurtures us and refuels us so we can shine brightly with energy and confidence.

We are wired to care for others to the point of feeling exhausted, depleted and tired. This is detrimental to our own health and wellbeing, and we end up feeling like a martyr and become resentful. Given that often our ever-growing to-do lists are virtually impossible to complete, this creates a recipe for igniting poor self-worth.

Self-care is tuning in and helping yourself before turning your attention to others. It's not about being self-absorbed or narcissistic, it's about getting in touch with ourselves, our wellbeing and our happiness, and showing up each day with a full tank. We practise self-love so we can push through our limiting beliefs and live a life that truly shines. To serve people in a healthy and sustainable way, we must put our own needs first. To sink into intimacy, we must honour ourselves first. To create a healthy family connection, we need to take care of our needs first. It's not selfish to put yourself first – it's vital.

Self-love is something to be encouraged because having a healthy attitude towards ourselves is better for everyone in the long run. We are able to give more love to others once we have given love to ourselves. We are able to be at peace with ourselves, receive love and find inner harmony, serenity and appreciation when self-care is practised.

Here are five ways to kickstart your pathway to success. Refuel and restore yourself with these self-care practices:

1. **STOP COMPARING YOURSELF** – Judging yourself against others is a neutraliser to self-love and depletes your energy.

2. **TAKE DAILY ACTION** – Address your basic needs. People high in self-love nourish themselves daily with healthy activities, clean nutrition, exercise, good sleep patterns, deep connection, respectful boundaries and healthy social interactions.

3. **BE GRATEFUL** – Take ten minutes every day to sit down, breathe deeply and think of all the amazing reasons to be happy.

4. **KEEP COMPLIMENTS ON FILE** – Chances are you can recall a negative comment someone said to you recently. Unfortunately our brains are not naturally programmed to remember the good comments. Support yourself and start a compliments file in the notes section of your phone. You can look at this on Monday mornings as a self-care ritual to begin the week.

5. **FORGIVE YOURSELF** – We are so hard on ourselves. To truly love yourself you have to acknowledge that no human is perfect. Mistakes are opportunities to learn and grow.

6. **CONNECT WITH THE MIRROR** – You are your best friend. Look at your best friend staring back at you with kindness, compassion and celebration. Acknowledge yourself each and every day.

Many of us have brilliant ideas daily, but because we spend so much time overthinking them, we fail to act upon them. Implementing guilt-free practices that boost your self-care is essential for your connection to self and others. From connection comes confidence. From permission comes freedom. It is about radiating who you really are and being proud of how you got to this chapter of your life. We can all make changes with small daily actions that align with our deepest desires and passions. These are acts of self-care.

SELF-CARE PRACTICES THAT CAN ALSO HELP TO SUPPORT YOUR SELF-LOVE

- **Own your inner and outer beauty** and compliment yourself without feeling guilty or entitled.
- **Buy yourself** flowers, just because.
- **Eat wholefoods** that make you feel vibrant and energised.
- **Make yourself** a cup of soothing herbal tea and dive into a good book.
- **Host** a dinner party.
- **Make yourself** a beautiful salad with every colour of the rainbow and tell yourself, 'This food is nourishing my body; it makes me feel alive.'
- **Give yourself** a foot massage with a botanical body cream.
- **Clean out** your wardrobe, give away one-third of your things and colour-coordinate the rest.

- ⊘ **Go** for a bushwalk, a swim, a spin class – just get out there. Exercise will release endorphins to make you feel good.
- ⊘ **Travel**. Anywhere. Just go and explore the world!
- ⊘ **Take** an Epsom salt bath.
- ⊘ **Book** a massage.
- ⊘ **Dab** some lavender essential oil on your wrists before bedtime.
- ⊘ **Go** to a morning yoga session.
- ⊘ **Take** a few deep, controlled breaths throughout the day to shake off any stress.
- ⊘ **Go** for a walk in nature.
- ⊘ **Enjoy** a comforting chai or hot chocolate.
- ⊘ **Listen** to your favourite podcast.
- ⊘ **Light** a candle and put on some classical or instrumental music.
- ⊘ **Meditate** on gratitude.

5

THE JOYOUS MASTER

Cultivate the habit
of being grateful
for every good
thing that comes
to you, and to
give thanks
continuously.

———

RALPH WALDO EMERSON

An attitude of gratitude means making a choice to express thankfulness and appreciation in all parts of your life on a regular basis, for both the big and small things. Having an attitude of gratitude is about choosing to appreciate and focus on what you have. As Oprah Winfrey says, 'Be thankful for what you have; you'll end up having more. If you concentrate on what you don't have, you will never, ever have enough.'

Usually when our energy is stuck, we experience the feeling that there isn't enough of something, whether it's money, time, love, friendships, compassion, health or understanding. The easiest way to get unstuck and back in the flow is through gratitude. The more we are drawn into the miserable stories and energy of those around us, the harder it is to connect with a deep sense of gratitude.

Some days, when you are feeling high on energy and health, you will see the world around you as an abundant tropical island full of gratitude. However, on days when you are low on sleep and feeling as if you are only just surviving, that tropical island may turn into a barren desert. On those days it is important that we take stock and remember that nothing has actually changed, only our perception of it. This is a time when a gratitude journal really earns its worth because you can flick back to see what you have previously been grateful for.

Recent studies show that feeling and expressing gratitude leads to better physical health, as well as improving your mood. Paul Mills, professor of Family Medicine and Public Health at the University of California's San Diego School of Medicine, conducted studies that looked at the role of gratitude on heart health. He found that participants who kept a journal most days of the week, writing about two to three things they were grateful for (everything from appreciating their children to travel and good food) had reduced levels of inflammation and improved heart rhythm, compared to people who did not write in a journal. The journal-keepers also showed a decreased risk of heart disease after only two months of this new routine!

For those people you know who always seem to be grateful and appreciative, theirs is an easy formula. A formula available to us all. Quite simply, their happiness is made possible by deliberately choosing to see the positive and connecting with their gratitude as many times as possible throughout the day. By doing this they create their own gratitude snowball that rolls down the mountain, growing larger with each positive affirmation.

Children are naturally happy and inquisitive. They have such a deep curiosity for small things and take pleasure in exploring the beauty and wonder of everything in front of them: the flower, the smile, the grass, the sky. They have full engagement in what they are doing. We can take wisdom from this simplicity and infuse our own daily routines with their sense of marvel. The ability to bring our attention to this present moment and truly connect with our appreciation will have us steeped in joy, wonder and beauty more often.

Practising gratitude doesn't require us to look far. Focus on the magic right in front of you by starting a daily gratitude journal. Your journal is your safe place to write, reflect and connect. Daily journalling also has incredible benefits for your health and wellbeing and will help you fill your tank of happiness, nurture your soul and refuel your energy stores.

FIVE BENEFITS OF BEING MORE GRATEFUL

1. **GRATITUDE** increases mental strength and helps to reduce stress.

2. **GRATITUDE** improves self-esteem – it helps us to stop judging ourselves and others.

3. **GRATEFUL** people sleep better – writing in your gratitude journal can help you to get your thoughts down on paper and sleep better.

4. **GRATITUDE** opens doors for more friendships – being thankful is magnetic.

5. **GRATITUDE** improves physical health – it helps you to value your health and therefore make good health a habit.

A gratitude journal is a tool for life – a tool that can become your best friend, the person you can tell anything and everything to. The simplest way to get started is to write down, morning and night, three things you are grateful for. Keep a little book next to your bed so it becomes a part of your morning and night-time routine.

THOUGHT-STARTERS TO BEGIN YOUR JOURNALLING

- Who do I appreciate?
- How am I fortunate?
- What material possessions am I thankful for?
- What abilities do I have that I'm grateful for?
- What about my surroundings (home/community/city) am I thankful for?
- What experiences have I had that I am grateful for?
- What happened today/yesterday/this week/this month that I am grateful for?
- What opportunities do I have that I am thankful for?
- What have people in my life done for me that I am thankful for?
- What relationships am I thankful for?
- What do I take for granted?
- What challenges/difficulties have I experienced (or am currently experiencing) that I can be thankful for?
- What have I learned? How have I grown?
- What changes am I thankful for that have occurred in the last year?
- What insights have I gained that I am grateful for?
- What am I able to offer others that I am grateful for?
- What opportunities to help others am I thankful for?

By the time you finish all the questions, you'll have a really clear picture of the gratitude in your life. You'll also have a great resource to go back to on those days when you're feeling a bit low on energy, zest and appreciation. Whether you choose to write a few sentences in a gratitude journal or simply take a moment to silently acknowledge all that you have, giving thanks can transform your life.

It's no wonder that some of the most successful entrepreneurs and thought leaders make gratitude a part of their routine. Sometimes it may feel a little forced, especially if you're frustrated, angry or miserable. But the more you practise and the more you look for things to be grateful for, the more that gratitude muscle grows and expands. It takes a bit of effort to get the muscle fit and lean, but having an attitude of gratitude is worth the effort as it is one of the most impactful habits for a fulfilling, happy and healthy life.

6

LIGHTEN AND
DECLUTTER

A tidy space isn't just about keeping things clean and organised but creating a space that improves your body and mind.

———

MARIE KONDO

Do your mind and body feel like a chaotic, fast-paced, emotionally fuelled, distracted, unconnected train wreck? Is your energy tank leaking at a faster pace than it can refuel itself?

If you desire clarity, serenity, energy and space, consider decluttering your environment. Clutter leads to stuck energy. It is toxic. Clutter is a dark cloud of weight that hangs around us day and night and stops our flow and our creativity. With clutter around us, our bright energy simply cannot shine. Overcrowding our lives with stuff leads to 'stuffocation', a feeling of being smothered by our possessions.

It's not just our homes that need decluttering – our minds do too. Too much racing around leads to exhaustion and a disconnection from self and inner harmony. Mental clutter can include worrying about the future, ruminating on the past, keeping a mental to-do list, negative self-talk, and even relentless, critical judgement of others.

When you feel overwhelmed and exhausted, it is time to simplify. It is your time now to realign yourself with what is essential and right for you, to prune the overgrowth and get back to what brings you joy and lets some light in. This will aid you to get back in touch with your true and authentic self. It will eliminate stress, allow you to create a vision and give you clarity and space.

Decluttering is an intentional process. It applies to your environment, your mind and your body. It allows you to find lightness, freedom and joy in your daily life. It is about letting go of all the noise, flirting with minimalism and creating a life of less stuff. It's about shifting old thoughts and feelings to live a life bursting with positive energy. When we talk of decluttering to restore ourselves, we need to think of both our inner and outer worlds.

You suffocate chi when you hoard objects and old thoughts or fail to thoroughly clean and respect your space.

If you are feeling overwhelmed, there are so many opportunities to get support. You can outsource some of these tasks and get help to make this a cathartic and exciting experience, rather than an all-encompassing, exhausting one. Letting go of excess creates joy. It creates space to breathe, to be, to find stillness, to refuel. It is a way of life, mentally, physically and emotionally. The space you will gain in your mind and environment will help you to restore yourself and get back to the basics, allowing you to shine, thrive and feel fulfilled by simple things. Our material possessions do not define who we are.

Every time you bring more stuff into your house, you should stop and ask questions, such as, 'Do I really want/need this?', 'Does it make me happy?' and 'Will I treasure this?'

Beware of re-cluttering – making space just to refill it with different stuff or new toxic thoughts. Physical clutter leads to mental clutter. We need to care more about what we do have and what is right for us. Your newly spacious surroundings and clearer mind will make you a better decision-maker.

Decluttering will also help your finances and give you a sense of freedom. When you shift into a more mindful mindset, you will take time to plan and, in the long run, purchase less and save more. You will start to pay attention to what your mind and body really need and what the cost is, either financially, emotionally or energetically. Mental clutter leads to congestion in our inner world. It gets in the way of thinking clearly and focusing on what really matters. Do we need to buy coffee every day? Do we need to keep buying clothes when we have a whole wardrobe full of outfits? Do we need to keep seeing the negative people in our lives who are drainers on our energy?

The simplest way to clean out our lives is to make it a fun activity with a time frame. Choose an area, clean it out and create some space. This new environment can restore you and help you feel your best.

Here are some areas to declutter that will soothe your soul and replenish your inner and outer worlds. Commit to one area at a time, take action, and feel the weight lift:

- Each room at home
- Finances
- Garden
- Car
- Technology

- Office
- Health
- Friendships
- Relationships
- Thoughts
- Attitudes
- Your routines and habits
- Your past

Commit to a daily decluttering routine with this powerful fast-track question in each area:

Are my current thoughts and actions serving my life's true purpose?

Once each area is decluttered, guard this state of being that you have created for yourself. There are so many free resources available on how to tackle each area individually. Become more minimal and find what your essential recipe is. This is your new way of living, to keep your tank full and your mindset positive so your environment is clear for abundant opportunity to flow.

7

PURIFY YOUR
THOUGHTS

You must weed
your mind as
you would weed
your garden.

———

ASTRID ALAUDA

Most of the time the thoughts we have are the same old limiting opinions and beliefs that keep us stuck where we are. Unless we are aware of the power of our thoughts and the need to plant positive seeds, our thoughts can hold us in a place of rumination, procrastination, fear or anxiety.

We all understand the benefits of looking after our bodies, but there is another important aspect of ourselves that we sometimes ignore – the health and agility of our minds. Unclogging, decluttering and cleansing your mind is just as important as keeping your body healthy. Many people try juice cleansing programs to eliminate toxins that they've accumulated over time. Just as we care for our bodies, we can also benefit from doing an intentional detox of our negative thoughts. See this as a rebooting of the hard drive. Our brains are like computers, and every year we could use a software upgrade. The World Health Organization predicts that work-related stress, burnout and depression will top the list of the world's most prevalent diseases by 2020.

It is the repetition of old, draining thoughts that keeps us imprisoned in the past. Think of this as your 'monkey mind' – a Buddhist term which refers to the constant, undirected thinking that often brings anxiety, worry and distraction into our everyday lives.

The continuous repetition of old thoughts and feelings rob us of new experiences. It also deprives us of bringing new possibilities into our lives. Just as a body detox involves draining your system of toxins and starting over with a healthy diet, a mental cleanse simply means draining toxic thoughts and replacing them with positive ones.

While most of us, at some point, take measures to clear the physical clutter in our homes, few of us ever pay the same attention to fighting the unnecessary junk cluttering up our minds. Many of us go through our lives without ever giving our minds a good clear-out and freshen-up, instead allowing old thoughts, concerns, beliefs, worries and irritations to influence our personalities.

We tend to dwell more on our negative thoughts than our positive ones, and the negative ones make a greater impact on our mental health. When you can intentionally tip the scale to the positive, you can gain more confidence, be more assertive and have a healthier mindset.

You know that old tape that runs in your head? It endlessly plays negative thoughts, like how overweight you are, how you could have done better in that presentation, how you may never get the job you want and how you are not smart enough or good enough. A mental cleanse helps you become aware of the negative self-talk and replace it with new positive and supportive thoughts.

The repetition of judgement and negative thinking is habit forming. If you repeat a behaviour over and over, you strengthen that neural pathway and it becomes the automatic route of choice. With practice you can learn to disrupt and tame negative cycles and build the muscle of positivity.

THE 7-DAY RECIPE FOR DETOXING YOUR MIND

DAY 1: INFLUENCED TO IMPACT – Unsubscribe from anything that drains your energy and your mind. Turn to those who make a positive impact on you instead. Only allow a stream of information from people you are motivated by and who inspire you to be the best version of yourself.

DAY 2: CLUTTERED TO CLEAR – Your physical surroundings impact how clear your thoughts are. Today take time to clear your desk and at least two cupboards at home. This will make a difference to your mind and your positivity.

DAY 3: OBSESSED TO DE-STRESSED – Learn how to end the obsession and breathe again. Take five minutes before you get out of bed and when you get into bed to belly-breathe. Feel the benefits of this calming breath.

DAY 4: OVERWHELMED TO OVERJOYED – Create space for you. Today is about organising a get-together with a group of friends who bring great meaning and energy into your life. This is an intentional get-together so you can practise creating positive conversation.

DAY 5: TRAPPED TO MAPPED – It's easy to get trapped in the past or stuck in a rut of mediocrity. Take time today to reignite your own personal vision and map out your goals until the end of the year. You should re-examine these on a weekly basis to stay on track.

DAY 6: STUMBLING TO SPRINTING – Plan your days effectively. Create a to-do list daily of three non-negotiables that you have set your mind on achieving and try to stick to it.

DAY 7: REACTIVE TO PROACTIVE – Act on your judgemental thoughts about yourself and others. Catch yourself today and use an affirmation to help train your mind to the positive.

Affirmations help purify our thoughts and restructure our brains so that we truly begin to think nothing is impossible. The word affirmation comes from the Latin *affirmare*, meaning 'to make steady' or 'strengthen'. Some thought-starters for your affirmations are:

- **I am** the architect of my life; I build its foundation and choose its contents.
- **Today** I am brimming with energy and overflowing with joy.
- **My body** is healthy; my mind is brilliant; my soul is tranquil.
- **I am** superior to negative thoughts and low actions.
- **I have** been given endless talents, which I begin to utilise today.

You can use any of these affirmations alone or create your own unique combination based on your personal dreams and desires. Affirmations are proven methods of self-improvement because of their ability to rewire our thought patterns. Much like exercise, they raise the level of feel-good hormones and push our brains to form new clusters of positive thought.

As you embark on any form of cleanse, there can be a feeling of sacrifice. This time that sacrifice is refraining from saying something negative or gossiping about someone or something. This is about changing your daily story. This cleanse is no different to a juice cleanse, cupboard declutter or garden overhaul. It is liberating to change your mindset. It is about setting yourself up for success and focusing on your '7-day recipe' to begin to change your thoughts, habits and outcomes. Focus on what you can control and create the thought patterns that give you a positive take on life.

8

FIRE UP YOUR CREATIVITY

Creativity involves breaking out of established patterns in order to look at things in a different way.

EDWARD DE BONO

The root meaning of the word creative is 'to grow'. When we allow creativity in, we find new ways to deal with obstacles and turn roadblocks into opportunities, rather than dead ends. By allowing ourselves to creatively view life from a different perspective or in a new way, we are able to then generate new possibilities or find alternatives to live a more exciting and energetic life. As you let creativity flow, you start to open up your heart and soul and treat life like a wonderful adventure. Kick-starting your creativity will take you from feeling exhausted to energised.

Creativity is a skill that needs constant nurture and exercise. When our tank feels depleted, firing up our creativity and opening the door to new solutions can be exciting and rewarding. Creativity is the ability to generate or recognise ideas, alternatives or possibilities that may be useful in solving problems, communicating and entertaining ourselves and others. A happy and fun-filled life requires creative thinking. Creativity triggers your courage as you allow yourself to try new things, become a little vulnerable, be brave and possibly fail.

In order to restore ourselves we need to find solutions to fill our depleted bodies, minds and souls, breathe life into our routines and turn the mundane into the magnificent. Creativity is linked to firing up our happiness, energy, tolerance, flexibility and enjoyment in life, both personally and professionally. When we are tired and rundown, our energy is at a low point and our creativity weakens. We then feel stuck in our problems, old habits, routines and relationships. This perception is draining and an exhausting way of living.

Focusing a little energy on seeing life through a new and creative lens can give us a way forward and can offer solutions to problematic situations. It can bring light to the dark and positivity to our fixed mindsets. It can offer a new perspective so we can flow again, create plans, movement and outcomes by seeing life in a new and brighter light.

Creativity will allow you to reconnect with what delights your soul, to create your dreams and visualise life in a lighter and more exciting way. It is finding joy in what you already do by tweaking your thoughts, routines and habits to fuel your internal fire. It is what will allow your life to become fun, energised and exciting each day. It is one of the most powerful life skills you can nurture, develop and harness. It will open the door to allowing yourself to find new and better ways to communicate with people, develop habits that serve you well and find more passion in life. The result is a restoration of your depleted energy.

We are all creative. We all have access to this incredible soul-nourishing part of us that often gets shut down when we are overloaded and overwhelmed. The great news is that we can reignite it at any time by putting in a little effort and creating a little space. Once we get it going, the rewards are amazing. We feel back in control, calm, confident and reconnected with our true selves. Actually following through to make change, we spark our imagination, which starts to fuel our creative outlook on life.

21 THOUGHT-STARTERS TO FIRE UP YOUR CREATIVITY

1. **CUT OUT PICTURES** to create a vision board for yourself and what you want to achieve in life.

2. **BOOST YOUR MOOD** by moving your body. Jump up and down, walk around the block, get some air to shift your brain state and kickstart your system.

3. **GO ON AN INSPIRATION TRAWL** by listening to TED Talks, audiobooks and podcasts on new topics.

4. **CONSTANTLY DOODLE** – Just let your pencil keep moving without judgement.

5. **LISTEN** to a different genre of music and be open to liking new sounds.

6. **KEEP A DREAM DIARY** – Dream wild and dream big and write it all down.

7. **COOK SOMETHING** with new flavours and styles.

8. **TRY A NEW HOBBY** – It can be anything, just start one.

9. **GO SOMEWHERE NEW** by trying a new route to work, a new lunch spot or a new coffee shop.

10. **GO OUT AND PLAY WITH YOUR PET** – Find the joy in creative play.

11. **GIVE YOURSELF PERMISSION** to fail and find laughter in your failure.

12. **SIT IN SILENCE AND WATCH PEOPLE** – See how wonderfully unique we all are.

13. **WRITE IN A JOURNAL EACH DAY** to clarify your thoughts, deepen your insight and understand your feelings.

14. **EXPERIENCE TEN MINUTES** a day of solitude and stillness to fully connect with yourself.

15. **HAVE** a picnic.

16. **GET UP** and watch the sunrise.

17. **BE A TOURIST** in your own home town.

18. **CHANGE** your hairstyle.

19. **TRY ON STYLES** of clothing you wouldn't normally wear.

20. **DINE** at a new restaurant.

21. **READ** philosophy.

IDEAS FOR STIMULATING CREATIVITY TO NURTURE YOURSELF

Create new routines to match the seasons – summer, autumn, winter, spring. Change the following with each season to keep your creativity alive:

- Overhaul your pantry and fridge on the first week of each season.
- Fine-tune your diet to eat seasonally.
- Adjust your exercise routine to work with the weather.
- Declutter and reset your wardrobe, bedroom and home environments.
- Book in some new activities for the 12-week cycle.
- Rewrite your affirmations to keep you motivated.
- Swap the colour of pen you use in your journal.
- Discover and program new meditations and intentions per season.
- Revamp your office and desk space.
- Organise seasonal catch-ups with friends.
- Every quarter, assess your daily media intake to ensure it continues to add value to your life.
- Choose new topics to learn and read about to enhance your skills.

Put a reminder in the calendar on the first day of each season to go through your checklist and create your seasonally adjusted goals.

Take note of how you feel when you ask yourself daily if you can do something better, make something more fun or build a deeper connection with someone. Empower yourself to use creativity to grow and flow. Capturing those moments, those experiences, those activities that take you closer to the flow state will allow you to truly flourish in life. Creativity is quite simply making fresh connections, showing up each day with a mind-set to see the world in a new way, try new things and be open to new perspectives.

9

STRENGTHEN
PATIENCE

Adopt the
pace of nature:
her secret
is patience.

———

RALPH WALDO EMERSON

Cultivating patience is more important now than ever before. We have all become programmed for instant gratification; we crave an instant life, fast results and surface-level interactions. Waiting for anything feels frustrating and annoying. Learning to be patient is a necessity to restore balance, to allow our minds and bodies to keep up, for our relationships to prosper and our careers to flourish.

Growing a baby takes time, losing weight takes time, becoming an elite athlete takes time, becoming a master in your field takes time, developing a deep connection in a relationship takes time, growing a healthy tree takes time, achieving a big goal takes time, healing a wound takes time, getting over loss takes time, life takes time. Give yourself some time.

Patience is the practice of living daily with calmness, even when presented with unpleasant circumstances. It is the ability to wait for something, to show restraint and give life's processes and projects time to fully develop. It is the ability to move over the speed bumps of life and continue on our journey without getting stuck.

In a distraction-filled environment where nothing gets considered properly, we jump from thought to thought, from worry to worry. We are living a life of interruption where we value entertainment over education. Our minds are in information overload. Patience requires you to take charge of your thoughts and words, which then dictate how you feel each day.

The key to a happy life is the ability to exercise patience in all areas. Some things need time. The path to great achievement is a long one, and those with no patience find it hard to stick to things because they want to see an instant result. To grow and learn, to keep on track with your goals, to save money and improve internal health – patience is our best and most powerful friend.

Remember how great it feels to have the patience to see a project through and tick it off your to-do list? The reason it feels so good is because whenever you recognise a task or project as being completed, your brain releases a hit of dopamine – a neurotransmitter that is responsible for generating feelings of accomplishment and satisfaction. This release of dopamine makes you feel happy and motivates you to continue completing tasks to extend that pleasant feeling. If we are low on patience, we can easily give up on our tasks part way through and end up with fragmented, half-completed projects. If you break up your goals into projects, your projects into tasks, and your tasks – if they are too large – into micro-tasks, you will have a list of things you can check off that will continuously provide you with energy and a sense of achievement. Ultimately you will conquer your goals.

Remember, we are human beings, not human doings. If we stop focusing on fast, instant results, we will have far greater success. Rome wasn't built in a day. Impatience is often a result of feeling out of control because you have overcommitted, overscheduled and overwhelmed yourself.

BENEFITS OF PATIENCE

- **Peace of mind** as you allow some breathing space in uncomfortable situations and thoughts.
- **Improved health** as we tend to make better lifestyle choices.
- **Achieved goals** as you stick to the long plan.
- **Improved relationships** as patience is a form of kindness and it promotes understanding, empathy and compassion, enabling us to comfort others.
- **Stronger mental health** as we navigate life's daily hassles, such as traffic and long queues, with less anger and irritation.
- **Better results** and fewer mistakes as you consider the bigger picture, assess problems and go through pros and cons.
- **Greater rewards** as you appreciate the process of growth, which takes planning and time.

17 SIMPLE WAYS TO CULTIVATE PATIENCE

1. **PRACTISE GRATITUDE** – For the big and small wins and for everything you have.

2. **LIVE WITH MINDFULNESS** – Allow yourself to feel what you are doing in the moment.

3. **REFRAME YOUR SITUATION** – Where is the opportunity for you to learn and grow?

4. **PAUSE TO NOTICE** – Every time you breathe in, notice there is fresh air for you.

5. **LET GO** of the tasks that are not essential.

6. **CHANGE YOUR ATTITUDE** – Get attached to the bigger picture and not the minute detail.

7. **SLOW DOWN** – Getting impatient does not make things move faster.

8. **THINK BEFORE YOU SPEAK** – Consider the consequences of what you are about to say.

9. **PRACTISE DELAYED GRATIFICATION** – Save yourself calories and money by thinking through your next choice.

10. **IDENTIFY YOUR TRIGGERS** and have a plan to deal with them.

11. **LEARN** to deep-breathe and melt your frustration away.

12. **TAKE TIME OUT** – Give yourself five minutes here and there to reset your expectations of yourself and others.

13. **VISUALISE YOURSELF AS A CALM**, confident and patient person.

14. **RECOGNISE** when you are being impatient and how you may be overreacting.

15. **MEDITATE** to nourish your heart and soul.

16. **STOP SWEATING THE SMALL STUFF** – Does it matter if it takes five minutes longer to complete a task?

17. **JUST LAUGH AND LOVE LIFE** – Lighten up, lean in and make it work for you.

Finally, remember that many of life's miracles do not happen quickly. They require patience; good things take time. Patience is a skill that can be mastered over time with practice. Don't miss out on the excitement and anticipation in the lead-up to getting that date, reaching that goal or taking that holiday. It is in this space that we flourish and treasure life. Master living in the now and find deep fulfilment in everyday life.

10

REVIVE WITH
YIN MOVEMENT

In the midst of movement and chaos, keep stillness inside of you.

— DEEPAK CHOPRA

Yin is our 'restorative energy'. It allows our mind and body to slow down, relax and rest. The concepts of yin and yang date back to ancient China. The symbol represents the belief that everything in the universe consists of two forces that are opposing but complementary. The yin is the female energy; it represents restorative and receptive energy. The yang is the masculine, action-focused energy. We need both the yang activity and the yin restfulness in life to stay healthy and balanced.

In a society that prides itself on achievements and busyness, it is increasingly important that we take time to balance these energies. In particular we need to replenish our yin energy. Yin energy encompasses the elements that nourish our body with things like sleep, concentration, focus and determination to follow our beliefs, morals, values and purpose. The simple act of working late and shaving time off your sleep will diminish your yin energy over time and will at some point need replenishing.

Slowing down and taking time to nourish yourself at every level will not only benefit your energy, your creativity and your mental/emotional balance, it will also benefit those around you. People who learn to rest deliberately can ultimately get more done for longer periods and find a deeper joy and meaning to their life.

You can exercise yin and yang polarities in all areas of life to maintain balance.

CONNECTING WITH YOURSELF

YANG: Be action-orientated and decisive. Have motivation, drive, focus and willpower.

YIN: Learn to relax and find a purpose. Make room for personal time to reflect and truly enjoy your life. Practise meditation, writing, prayer and connecting with nature.

CONNECTING WITH OTHERS

YANG: Practise being sociable, personable and extroverted. Speak to others, reach out to them and share.

YIN: Be perceptive. Listen and be thoughtful, compassionate, empathetic and understanding. Turn inward, receive, build rapport, take time to communicate and build trust with others.

EXERCISE

YANG: Yang exercises are quite intense in nature and usually result in muscle fatigue. Good examples include weight-lifting, competitive contact sports, circuit training and power yoga.

YIN: Yin exercises tend to leave you feeling rejuvenated, rather than depleted. Practices like yin yoga, Pilates, tai chi, qi gong, stretching, foam rolling, Feldenkrais and some forms of dance and martial arts are some examples – all of which require full participation of body, mind and spirit. Presence and attention are key aspects of this approach, making a yin-style training session not just a workout for your body, but for your brain and nervous system as well. Yin yoga is particularly beneficial to those who participate regularly in yang activities as it provides a counterbalance. While yin yoga is slow, it is not restorative yoga, which is a completely different but equally beneficial style. Positions in yin are held anywhere from one to 20 minutes and so can be quite challenging, both physically and mentally.

You can think of these balancing exercises as a way of attracting opposites. Remember to monitor yourself and make conscious efforts to keep yourself aligned by equally concentrating on both energies. When our attention is focused on just one energy, we become worn-out and it's hard to effectively manage our lives. Keeping our lives balanced with yin and yang energy allows us to easily navigate through life events, making us more adaptable and resourceful human beings.

HERE ARE SOME LIFESTYLE CHANGES TO NOURISH THE YIN

- Fall asleep before 10 pm.
- Sleep in a very dark room on an empty stomach.
- Limit screen time during the day, avoid it after 5 pm.
- Avoid rushing.
- Take a power nap when you need to.
- Hydrate the body with water, limit caffeine and eliminate soft drinks.
- Eat a wholefood diet (organic dairy or dairy substitute, vegetables, grains, legumes, good oils, nuts and locally sourced meat or meat substitutes).
- Surround yourself with people you love.
- Limit fearful moments (watching scary movies, driving in intense weather, being in crowded or loud places).
- Commute by walking or riding your bicycle.
- Grow some of your own food or go to farmers' markets.
- Be in nature every day.
- Participate in slow-moving or still activities.
- Meditate.

- Ø Create moments without any activity at all to experience stillness.
- Ø Create firewalls between work and home: transition consciously so that you don't take work home.
- Ø Stay fully in the present moment by practising mindfulness.
- Ø Practise gratitude.
- Ø Stay at home in the evening hours.
- Ø Attend a weekly yin yoga class.

We can nourish yin throughout the day by taking micro pauses – paying attention to our breath at traffic lights, pausing before we eat, offering ourselves a compassionate inner dialogue. These little things add up over time and will support the harmony of yin and yang, which is the basis for our happiness and health. Embrace the yin, the stillness and the quiet, to restore yourself and find harmony.

11

EMBRACE
TECHNOLOGY

Once I was
a scuba diver
in a sea of words.
Now I zip along
the surface like a
guy on a jet ski.

———

NICHOLAS CARR

Technology is both freedom and a ball and chain. It keeps us connected and yet lonely. It is amazing and addictive.

Technology is here to stay so it's time to embrace it with a positive mindset and utilise it so it works for us rather than against us. It is a powerful daily relationship we can foster, to harness and capture, to interact wisely with, to be in control of and use as a part of our restorative journey. Technology can support peace and inner harmony if we use it well.

Heavy technology usage negatively impacts our self-esteem, sleep, relationships, identity, empathy and patience, resulting in impulsive behaviours, stress, anxiety and depression. We become fatigued with mindless swiping, obsessively checking social media every five minutes for fear of missing out. We also secure a toxic judgement practice like never before. No wonder so many people are in a stuck, tired and sad state.

The exciting part is that we can jump back in the control seat and leverage and customise our technology to support us, work for us and guide us to success. With a little planning, effort and execution, we can program technology to be our servant. It is time to make it work for us. People need less stress and more quiet time, family time and personal time, and this is possible if we learn how to reprogram and unplug. Creating great relationships that fill our lives with incredible joy, depth and warmth is what makes people happy, and technology can educate us and connect us like never before.

Technology is amazing at bringing people together with Skype, text, email and FaceTime. It can work as an exercise incentive, remind you to breathe and pause, offer incredible access to guided meditations from teachers globally, and monitor your goals. We can shop online to avoid traffic, queues and waiting, and we no longer have to leave home to pay our bills.

But technology is just a means to an end. It is not an end. It is our attitude and ability to program it and understand the impact it is having on our lives that will free us and take us to new heights. Your technology choices must work for you and help you win where it matters. Every minute you spend pointlessly on your phone is a minute taken away from time spent with your family and friends, on your health, your hobbies, and in stillness, which are at the base of your best self, your most restored, energetic and vibrant self.

So, get back in control by following these simple steps.

GET IN TOUCH WITH HOW YOU ARE USING YOUR TECHNOLOGY

- What features make you feel good?
- What time limits have you set for yourself?
- What part of technology is robbing you of time that could be spent on self-care, goals and preparation for success?
- How is it impacting your sleep?
- Is it topping up your happiness tank?
- Are you comfortable having a day without technology?

MAKE THE CHANGES

- Set technology boundaries, such as no technology after 9 pm and before 7 am to control your usage.
- Remove your phone from the bedroom and buy an alarm clock.
- Switch off your mobile phone at night but keep a landline so people can still contact you in an emergency.
- Use your calendar as a guide to write down your daily to-do list for the next day.
- If you need help remembering to switch off your devices, set your alarm at 9 pm as a reminder. Before long you will not need the alarm at all.
- Remove all app alerts from your phone.
- Cull your apps – delete all the apps you do not use. If you need them in the future you can reinstall them.
- Put your social media apps on the last page on your phone or limit yourself to using only one type of social media. Do you need to have them all?
- Turn on the 'do not disturb' button when you need space or are working on a project.
- Turn email off on your phone – you will survive.
- Clean out your computer, smart phone or tablet quarterly.
- Ensure that all your technology devices talk to each other and sync to avoid frustration.

EDUCATE YOURSELF ON HOW HIGHLY EFFECTIVE PEOPLE USE THEIR TECHNOLOGY

How to Break Up with Your Phone author Catherine Price describes the 7 phone habits of highly effective people as:

1. **A HEALTHY PHONE ROUTINE** – Where do you charge your phone? Where do you keep it while at work, at home, at dinner?

2. **PHONE MANNERS** – When eating a meal, your phone should be out of sight. When driving a car: no way, no question. In classes and movies, it should be muted. Ditto when working on tasks and goals.

3. **ALLOW A BREAK** – Regularly give yourself small amounts of guilt-free phone time.

4. **PHAST (PHONE FASTING)** – No phones when travelling, reading, writing, cooking and doing activities you want to fully enjoy without disruption.

5. **HAVE A LIFE** – Enjoy hobbies, dinner parties with no phones, exercising with friends.

6. **PRACTISE PAUSING** – Moments of stillness, observation and silence instead of reaching for your phone to fill the time.

7. **EXERCISE ATTENTION** – Focus on an activity to build attention, such as meditation or finishing a project; complete tasks without the distraction of a phone.

Remember, technology is here to make your life better. If it is not and you are feeling depleted, disorganised and exhausted, it is time to take some control back and become the master.

12

DEVELOP
FORGIVENESS

It's one of the greatest gifts you can give yourself, to forgive. Forgive everybody.

———

MAYA ANGELOU

Forgiveness is defined as a conscious, deliberate decision to release feelings of resentment or vengeance towards a person or group who has harmed you, regardless of whether they actually deserve your forgiveness. This practice can set you free. It allows you to let go and see those life experiences as a part of you that made you stronger. This is a ritual that will restore your life, clean the slate and allow you to move forward.

It does not mean forgetting and moving on, condoning bad behaviour or glossing over events that have caused you grief. Rather it involves the practice of letting go of deep negative and angry feelings that are harming you. It is an act of kindness towards yourself to forgive others. Your experience with someone from the past is now just a thought or feeling that you are carrying around with you which takes the nourishment out of your heart. Resentment, hatred and anger debilitate your energy flow and disempower you. These thoughts and feelings are a ball and chain. When you opt for forgiveness, it is an act of self-love.

Self-forgiveness is critical to our wellbeing and health. It is a personal act of humility, to be honest and acknowledge where we may have let ourselves or others down. It offers us the chance to turn the table, move forward and take responsibility for our actions. In so many situations we fail to do this and harbour destructive thoughts. In some cases we may have made many of the choices that resulted in a situation we were not happy with. Our experience is generally one of guilt and shame, from hurting others, becoming self-critical, self-sabotaging with food, collecting negative thoughts, breaking rules, betraying loved ones or an addiction to perfectionism.

Self-forgiveness is not about letting yourself get away with things, but rather opening the door to an opportunity to change behaviours, get help, accept what has happened, say you're sorry, own up to mistakes and create change. Forgiveness is a part of healing that comes from within and can take a long time. In some cases, forgiveness is not possible. And this is okay as you honour your life and the events that have occurred. It is about taking small steps to take action and give you back some time to make a positive difference in your life. When you move into self-forgiveness you move towards acceptance. A person who practises self-acceptance is someone who experiences challenges and accepts failure and unhappiness as a part of life. You can't grow without forgiveness. But know that it's a process and it will take time. Forgive others for things they didn't mean to do. Forgive others for things they didn't know they did. Forgive yourself for mistakes you think you've made. And forgive yourself if things don't change quickly enough.

SOME SIMPLE QUESTIONS TO ASK YOURSELF

- ∅ Have I forgiven myself or others?
- ∅ What is not forgiving myself or others costing me?
- ∅ What are the benefits of forgiveness in this situation?
- ∅ What am I fighting for – my ego or the greater good?

Forgiveness of self and others allows us to redirect that all-consuming energy of anger, holding grudges, sadness, shame, guilt and resentment towards learning new ways and refocusing on our self-care, growth, vision and goals. It is about choosing peace and inner harmony over being right. It is about cleaning out our outdated thoughts, patterns, reactions and behaviours that no longer serve us, and nourishing our heart, soul and energy reserves.

TIPS TO START THE FORGIVENESS PROCESS

- *Ø* **Acknowledge** that forgiving someone or yourself is about freeing you to move forward.
- *Ø* **Accept** that your life to date is the story of your past; it doesn't have to be the story of your future. Acceptance is the key to starting any new process or habit when we want to create change.
- *Ø* **Write** a letter and burn it (instead of sending it) to get all your thoughts and anger out.
- *Ø* **Develop** empathy because most people are just trying to do their best and there are always circumstances that you are not aware of.
- *Ø* **Understand** that this is about taking responsibility in order to move forward in life.
- *Ø* **Try** to find meaning and purpose in what you have experienced.
- *Ø* **Find** the opportunity for your actions, or the actions of others, to apply to your life now.
- *Ø* **Know** that you too may have played a part, so start earning forgiveness from others by making amends, saying a heartfelt sorry and seeking support.

Remember, forgiveness takes courage and strength. It will set you free. It might not always be easy to forgive yourself or others, but the benefits are big. Without acceptance and forgiveness, we cannot move forward.

When you forgive, be sure to really forgive and don't rehash the past. Do it once, commit to it and let it be gone. You are capable of accomplishing great things. Believe that you can do anything – because you can. You are a strong and powerful being and you can deal with any challenge that comes your way.

The weak can never forgive. Forgiveness is the attribute of the strong.

———

MAHATMA GANDHI

13

AWAKEN YOUR
DREAMS

Shoot for the moon.
Even if you miss,
you will land
among the stars.

———

LES BROWN

Dreams bring us life, energy, joy, hope and determination. Dreams fuel our success. They are at the soul of who we are and give us a great sense of purpose, direction and meaning in life. Allowing yourself to start dreaming will bring your imagination, inspiration and motivation to life once again. It does not matter how old or young you may be or what you do for a living, dreams offer hope and a pathway to set goals.

What is your dream? What do you want to chase and what do you want to achieve?

Dreaming allows you to think big and harness something improved for yourself. It loads up your ideas tank and sparks the fire within your soul. They are not just flights of your imagination with no purpose, they are a vital part of who we are and they allow us to grow and evolve, and give us incredible energy and power. To turn our thoughts into reality, we need to dream big and set our minds on a course that supports those dreams.

Behind every successful person there is a dream fulfilled. There has been something that as a child, teen or adult they have focused on and achieved. Something that fired them up, got them motivated, excited and even captivated them. Their dreams became goals with deadlines.

Our dreams are constantly evolving. Oprah Winfrey once said in an interview, 'The truth is that I never set out to create this huge life. The path to my success was never about attaining incredible wealth or celebrity. It was about the process of continually seeking to be better, challenging myself to pursue excellence on every level.'

As life gets busier and our energy gets stuck in a rut, we feel the mundaneness of daily life and we forget to dream. We forget what we are passionate about, what excites us, and lose touch with what we really love to do.

To start dreaming, we ask small, powerful questions to tap into understanding who we are and what inspires us. We shut down some of the noise to ponder what course we want to set, what we can imagine for ourselves and how to create a wonderful life based on our own set of values and priorities in life.

QUESTIONS TO PUT YOUR DREAMS INTO ACTION

1 – RECONNECT WITH WHO YOU ARE

- What do you love to do?
- What do you love spending your time on?
- What experiences fill your soul with joy?
- What do you love learning about?
- What does your perfect day look like?
- What aspects of your life today do you want more of?

2 – GET YOUR DREAM ON AND CAPTURE YOUR ANSWERS ON PAPER

- How do you feel when you wake up?
- Where do you want to travel?
- What topics do you love talking about?
- What is most important to you?
- What are you passionate about?
- What do you want to spend money on?
- What is your dream job?
- What events do you want to attend?
- What life experiences do you want to capture?

- What do you want to create for your physical, mental and emotional health?
- What would you do if money was not an issue?

Think big, create and embrace these answers. Prioritise them and capture them on paper. This is how we get into designing our life, rather than living by default. This is how we turn the mundane into the magnificent. This is what ignites the soul and gives light to a life of maximum fulfilment. Taking the time to let our dreams run wild is as liberating as being let loose in the playground.

3 – FINE-TUNE YOUR IMAGINATION

- Dream for three, five and ten years in the main quadrants of life.
- Health – body, mind, energy, self-love, fitness, nutrition. How do you want to feel?
- Relationships – partner, children, friends, family, mentors. What connections do you want to embrace?
- Career – mentors, promotions, sabbaticals, networks, skill sets. What do you want to achieve?
- Finances – security, assets, financial pathways, retirement, investments, giving back. What is your base and structure for choice in life?
- Education – student for life, becoming an expert, crafting a hobby, deepening your knowledge. What do you want to learn?

4 – CREATE SOLUTIONS TO ACHIEVE YOUR DREAM

- Optimistically believe in your dreams.
- Create a mind-map of your dreams.
- Define what you need to let go of to allow your dreams to evolve.
- Find the strength and courage to develop goals.
- Create solutions to remove the roadblocks.
- Break your three-year plan into small steps with realistic goals.
- Co-create and dream with other positive people; let them be your cheerleaders.
- Allow a few moments each day to connect with your sense of freedom and allow yourself to dream.

Remember, goals are dreams with time frames and deadlines. Let go of false limitations, get organised, believe in yourself, plan, listen, inject some passion and allow the flow. With a healthy dose of self-care, belief and support, we can restore ourselves, get our energy flowing and brighten our souls. Each day is a new day. It is never too late to start a dream, a goal, a project or learn something new.

DREAM IDEAS

- Live next to the beach
- Grow my own vegetables
- Travel the world
- Love deeply
- Learn an instrument
- Find inner harmony
- Write a book
- Feel strong and agile
- Live with joy
- Make new friends
- Kiss in the rain
- Run a marathon
- Be debt-free
- Feel confident
- Master cooking
- Have great posture
- Meditate daily

14

REFRESH WITH THE SENSES

Memories establish the past; senses perceive the present; imaginations shape the future.

———

TOBA BETA

Having a supercharged sense of smell, sound, sight, taste and touch can transform your everyday life. It is predominantly through the five senses that we come to experience all the dimensions of the world and its wonder.

Our senses are our gateway to the present moment. In fact, according to recent studies there are anywhere from 11–21 different senses that we use every single day. At times these senses go overlooked and unnoticed; however, there are five basic sensory systems that support us on a daily basis.

Our sensory information streams are vital for our protection and survival, and they serve as our most basic form of communication. In relation to our wellbeing, this means understanding our senses and using them more creatively and proactively to harness their full potential.

One of the most effective ways we can feel more connected and energised is by tuning in to our senses. We tend to take them for granted when we are busy. Rushing from one task to the next, constantly bombarded with noise and stimulation, it's easy for our senses to become dulled. This leads to a more lacklustre life, where countless opportunities for joy and appreciation are missed because we aren't aware of them.

FIVE SUPERCHARGED STRATEGIES FOR YOUR SENSES

1. **TASTE** – Whenever you are eating or drinking, focus on the taste of the food or beverage. Is it bitter, sweet, salty or spicy? Being mindful when you are eating will help aid your digestion and enrich your experience.

2. **SIGHT** – Leave your phone at home and take a walk. So many of us walk with our heads down, buried in our thoughts, without even realising it. Look up to the beautiful horizon, the nature around you and the people you pass on the street.

3. **SOUND** – Close your eyes and allow yourself to connect to all of the sounds around you: the children playing, the crashing ocean, the whirl of the wind, the rustle of dry leaves, the overheard conversations, the birds in the distance. Immerse yourself in all of the sounds that surround you, rather than selectively hearing only one.

4. **TOUCH** – Practise becoming aware of anything that is coming into contact with your body, from the warmth of the sun on your face, to the texture of the grass beneath your bare feet. Feel the fabric of your clothes touching your skin. You can also regularly apply your favourite hand cream or body cream throughout the day to keep you connected to your sense of touch, or better yet, book a monthly massage.

5. **SMELL** – Take time to appreciate the smell of the ocean, the aroma of coffee roasting, hot bread wafting from the bakery, freshly cut grass, sliced watermelon on a summer's day, or a lit candle.

We can also use essential oils to help strengthen and sharpen our sense of smell. The optimum way for the body to benefit from the therapeutic qualities of essential oils is through a combination of inhalation and skin absorption. When you are inhaling essential oils, it takes 22 seconds for the the oil to reach your brain. Sometimes when you apply an oil to the skin, it almost seems to disappear into the body. When applied topically, it takes two to three minutes for an oil to reach the bloodstream, 20 minutes to affect every cell in the body and two and a half hours for it to then be metabolised.

You can use essential oils in an oil diffuser, roll-ons, body oils, bath oils, or even try sprinkling it on the floor of your shower to make an aroma shower. Keep in mind that perfume oils are different from essential oils and don't offer the same therapeutic benefits.

FIVE ESSENTIAL OILS THAT YOU CAN USE EVERY DAY

1. **LAVENDER OIL** – Calms and relaxes, relieves anxiety, improves sleep, alleviates skin rashes, acne, insect bites and minor burns.

2. **LEMON OIL** – Increases mood and concentration, reduces fevers, infections, asthma, skin disorders, hair conditions, stomach problems and tiredness.

3. **PEPPERMINT OIL** – Boosts energy levels, improves focus, supports healthier digestion, reduces fever and headaches, and provides muscle pain relief.

4. **TEA TREE OIL** – Treats dermatitis, eczema, cold sores, nail fungus and warts and can be used as a disinfectant spray.

5. **EUCALYPTUS OIL** – Improves sinusitis, bronchitis, allergies, reduces congestion, increases mental clarity, as well as being a natural disinfectant.

Sensory meditation uses one or many of the five senses – listening to sounds, soft gazing, inhaling aromas, feeling with your hands or other body parts, and focused tasting – to fully experience the present moment. The senses become a channel for all the information coming into your body, and all of your thoughts surrender to the precious present moment as it unfolds.

If you're having a bad day, one surprisingly quick and effective way of de-stressing is to deliberately turn your attention to any of the five senses. A shift will occur in your brain quite quickly and you'll start to relax. This simple strategy – shifting from thinking to sensing – is the essential ingredient in nearly all meditation practices. Note that this is NOT a shift away from thinking. It's a shift towards sensing.

Grounding yourself with these daily rituals will allow you to relish the present moment. The impacts on your mind and your body are highly beneficial. You don't always need a meditation pillow or a mantra to practise mindfulness. Simply allow your body to receive the abundant gifts that surround us each moment by tuning in to your senses.

15

HEALING
THROUGH FOOD

The food you eat
can be either
the safest and most
powerful form
of medicine or
the slowest form
of poison.

————

ANN WIGMORE

Life's simplest pleasures are the best ones, and food is no exception. Food is our ultimate pleasure – it can boost our energy, our mood and our health. The food you eat today will determine your health tomorrow. Every time you eat, it's an act of self-care. Everything you put into your body is a choice. Food is nourishment.

These days, however, we often find ourselves eating on the run, compromising the way we eat and the quality of what we eat. The instant way of eating is negatively impacting our health and digestive systems. Currently one in five Australian women suffer from Irritable Bowel Syndrome. It is a sign that our guts are inflamed and we need to listen to our bodies more. Hippocrates (460–370 BCE), the father of modern medicine, declared that, 'All disease begins in the gut.' The gut is our foundation for optimum health and wellbeing. Our food has the ability to harm us, heal us, energise us and nourish our exhausted bodies. As Hippocrates also said, 'Let food be thy medicine, and medicine be thy food.' We can learn from his wise words all these years later.

Athletes choose food for ultimate body and mind performance. Every day we want more capacity, more energy, more patience, more compassion, more love and more happiness. This requires fuel, and the better the fuel, the better results. If you want a Formula One performance from your body, what are you putting in? How are you refuelling?

We make choices every day that either support or deteriorate our health and wellbeing. When you open your fridge and look at the food you have inside, does it give you a high 'return on ingestion'? Does it give you the right energy? These are the questions we need to ask ourselves.

A HEALTHY DIET CAN HELP

- Increase productivity and concentration
- Reduce inflammation
- Optimise energy levels
- Regulate weight
- Give you glowing skin, healthier hair, stronger nails
- Reduce cravings
- Improve sleep
- Add years to your life by reducing your risk of stroke, heart disease, diabetes, certain cancers and much more

A wholefood eating plan helps ensure that your entire body gets the nutrition it requires. That's because wholefoods carry out the major functions of a good diet, which include absorption, assimilation and elimination – everything a healthy body needs.

Eating well means making daily choices to leave out, or rarely eat, foods that are high in added sugar, saturated fat and sodium. That includes most fast foods, soft drinks and processed snacks such as chips, crackers, biscuits and cakes. Start small by replacing one of these food items with a better alternative for one month. Once you master one vice, move on to the next. By the end of the year you will have eliminated 12 unhealthy items from your diet.

The more you eat,
the less flavour;
the less you eat,
the more flavour.

———

CHINESE PROVERB

TOP TIPS FOR NOURISHING FOOD CHOICES

- Order groceries online so you aren't tempted to put chocolate bars in your trolley.
- Drink water first thing in the morning.
- Have lemon slices in your water to stimulate your digestion.
- Say 'no' to second helpings.
- Don't put sugar in hot drinks.
- Shop the outside aisles of the supermarket.
- Don't buy foods with more than five ingredients on the label.
- Aim for the half-plate rule with every meal (one half fruit and veg and the other half protein and/or carbohydrates).
- Incorporate wholefoods in cooking wherever possible.
- Always have breakfast.
- Snack on fresh fruit or raw nuts in between meals.
- Reduce your unhealthy habits by committing to a structure that supports your health: for example, limiting chocolate and wine to weekends only.
- Moderation is key.
- Prepare healthy meals ahead of time and keep them in your freezer.

- Have fun and get creative with how you serve your meals.
- Try a new recipe once a month.
- Turn the TV off while you have dinner to avoid overeating while distracted.
- Avoid having devices at the dinner table, so you can have connected conversations.
- Ask yourself before you eat something, 'Will this nourish me?'
- Every now and again treat yourself to a little dark chocolate (minimum 70 per cent cocoa).

Keep in mind that good choices, like eating a healthy diet, happen one step at a time. A few small changes can help improve your life right now. Create the structure for you to transition into your new eating routine one day, one habit and one choice at a time. Pace yourself, and if you find yourself getting off track, remember that tomorrow is a new day and a great opportunity to reset. This is what nourishing our body, mind and spirit is all about.

16

REKINDLE
FRIENDSHIPS

Having strong social bonds is probably the most meaningful contributor to happiness.

———

GRETCHEN RUBIN,
AUTHOR OF *THE HAPPINESS PROJECT*

Friendships enrich us and are a vital element of our health and wellbeing. Friends support us, inspire us, teach us, help us cope with challenges and share in our great celebrations. We often underestimate the impact our closest relationships and social connections have on our wellbeing. Our lives can become richer, more vibrant and energetic with a few soul-nourishing friends.

Human beings adopted group living as a primary solution to the problem of survival. Alone, life can feel intolerable and our health and longevity suffer. Real-life connections between human beings are what give us confidence, drive, energy, courage, strength and joy. We are social creatures. We need other people in our lives to be happy, and even to be healthy.

Our connections suffer when we are tired, exhausted and allow technology to replace our real-life friendships. While technology is amazing at keeping us connected, especially with long-distance family and friends, we need to rekindle our real-life friendships and savour them. Most of us can trace our successes to pivotal relationships and see that our lives have been constructed through these interactions and experiences.

THE MAIN BENEFITS OF FRIENDSHIPS

THEY KEEP US PHYSICALLY AND MENTALLY STRONG. They help us deal with stress, make better lifestyle choices and assist us when we are ill.

THEY SUPPORT US IN SAD AND LONELY TIMES by offering kindness, acceptance and comfort.

THEY HELP US GROW AND IMPROVE our interactions, with laughter, conversation, knowledge and forgiveness.

THEY DEEPEN OUR QUALITY OF LIFE by giving more meaning to our experiences. They fill us with gratitude, happiness and love of life, and they create connections in our community.

From the moment we stepped into the playground, friendships became a fundamental part of our life. We developed our social fingerprint (how often we prefer social contact) and experienced the turbulence as friendships changed and evolved. We also experienced the effect romantic relationships had on our friendships.

THERE ARE THREE TYPES OF FRIENDS

1. **THE FRIENDS THAT COME AND GO** – Hello and goodbye, these are acquaintances.

2. **REGULAR CATCH-UP FRIENDS** – Our community, school, workplace or activity buddies that we can talk to about our general day-to-day life.

3. **TRUE SOULMATES** – Real friends, who do not judge us, will go the extra mile and are there for us in the long run.

In today's society, the average ratio for the three types of friend is said to be 75-20-5 per cent. Study after study shows that if we have one to five friends who don't judge us, who are there for us in both good and bad times and who understand us, then we are likely to live longer and have much richer lives. It is also said that we are the average of the five people we spend the most time with. We are greatly influenced by those closest to us. Are these people inspiring and supportive? Are they helping you grow or are they anchors holding you down? Think of the compound effect people have on you and find clarity in what you want to create for yourself in the future.

If you remember people, they will remember you. To restore yourself and bring back the energy of connection into your life, rekindle old positive friendships, create new ones and move away from the toxic ones. This will inspire you once again and give you a whole-hearted feeling of belonging. Our friendships often determine our level of happiness. When you reflect on the most memorable events, experiences and moments in your life, both of utter joy or broken-heartedness, you'll notice that they have something in common: the presence of another person. The best moments – and most of the agonising ones – occur at the intersection of two people.

When igniting and making new friends, remember you become who you hang out with. Invite new people in who inspire you, who will challenge you, who will take you to new heights, who will push you and may even dream with you.

THOUGHTS TO IGNITE AND ENRICH OUR FRIENDSHIPS

- Learn to forgive
- Listen more, talk less
- Avoid judgement of others
- Make friendships a priority
- Embrace quality and ditch quantity
- Ride out the transitions people go through
- Make the effort and commitment to build friendships
- Find new like-minded people with similar interests to connect with
- Develop momentum by booking in regular catch-ups or phone calls
- Let go of toxic relationships and draining people
- Accept new invitations
- Ask interesting questions to develop a greater understanding
- Get to know your friends' friends
- Join a new group, book club or hobby group
- Take the first step and say hello; be interested in people
- Be open to new people and foster new connections
- Connect with warmth, respect and interest
- Be your true self

- Remember birthdays
- Get to know your neighbour
- Throw a dinner party
- Exercise with friends
- Talk about ideas, not other people

Those who make a deliberate effort to foster and nurture their friendships and networks have high social wellbeing – they will travel with friends, make time for social gatherings and one-on-one connections and enjoy long conversations with people. This creates joy.

Solid friendships with memories and history create a familiarity in life which is safe and comforting to the soul. They provide a sense of belonging and are an integral part of our overall feeling of wellbeing.

17

BATHE
IN NATURE

Look deep into nature, and then you will understand everything better.

ALBERT EINSTEIN

Nature is freedom; nature is connection. Nature is the ocean that stretches to the horizon and the lush tropical valley that travels as far as the eye can see. Nature offers us one of the most reliable boosts to our mental and physical wellbeing. Spending time outside opens your mind and sharpens your thinking.

Nature shows us that there is no such thing as perfection. There is no perfect tree or perfect flower, yet they are all beautiful, and we accept and love that. When we are in the natural world, we are more accepting of our surroundings and therefore more accepting of ourselves. We take the pressure off ourselves and bathe in the beauty that surrounds us. This is nourishing for our minds, and the more we take a moment to pause in nature, the more we replenish our precious bodies, minds and souls.

Our modern lifestyle has led us to spend more time inside, and as much as we know it's good to get outside for that much-needed fresh air and vitamin D, sometimes the lure of the couch at the end of a long afternoon is too tempting, and suddenly just the thought of going for a walk outside can seem exhausting. Getting away from big buildings, technology and noise on a regular basis makes you happier, more at peace and grounded. We need space. When we get out in nature, we are prompted to listen to our bodies and find a natural rhythm to match our surroundings. Urgency, deadlines and time melt away. Instead we are guided by the sun rising and setting and the innate beauty of the changing seasons. Once we make the effort to get out in nature, time slows down and we can see that adaptability is the key to success. No day is identical. No weather pattern is the same, and nature flows with it all.

Scientists are beginning to find evidence that being in nature has a profound impact on our brains, helping to reduce anxiety, brooding and stress, and increase our attention capacity, our creativity and our ability to connect with other people. Make it a promise to yourself to spend more time in nature. Exercise outside instead of going to the gym, read outdoors, organise weekend getaways in nature, take your shoes off and walk barefoot. At the very least, get a plant for your office. Live your best life by spending more time in nature.

20 TOP WAYS TO GET BACK IN NATURE

- Gaze at the night sky, look at the stars.
- Relax on a park bench, Forrest Gump-style.
- Look for shapes and objects in the clouds.
- Watch a sunrise, sunset or both.
- Get back into loving your garden, plant your own vegetables.
- Listen to night sounds like crickets chirping.
- Do yoga poses outside.
- Visit a nearby river or creek, or park with fountains, and listen to the water flow.
- Have a picnic in a public garden.
- Look for four-leaf clovers with your children.
- Book an outdoor rock climbing, kayaking or sailing lesson.
- Participate in a community clean-up project.
- Hike somewhere you have never been before.
- Take a walk in your neighbourhood, stopping to talk to your neighbours.
- Take photos of nature and put them around your desk or in your diary.
- Watch the moon go through its phases.

- ∅ Walk through a park to work.
- ∅ Take your lunchbreak in a park.
- ∅ Plan holidays in nature.

One way to get the most out of our connection to nature is to take a moment to acknowledge sensations. We can stop and think about the feeling of the cool air on our skin, the fresh scents we smell, the vibrancy of colours and organic shapes we see, the relaxing sounds we hear and the variety of textures around us. We can take a minute to put our hands on the soft moss, the smooth bark of a tree or let sand run through our fingers. We can take off our shoes and feel the ground beneath our feet, bringing our attention to whether it feels hard or soft, cool or warm, damp or dry. This is called 'being present'. It is a form of meditation. Everyone's access to nature is different, but it is worth taking the opportunities to connect with nature whenever we can. Nature is magic. Nature is free. Nature helps to top up our tank and gives us space, and that space helps to park our worries and reconnect to what helps us to live lives of meaning and joy.

18

INVEST IN
LEARNING

Live as if you were
to die tomorrow.
Learn as if you
were to live forever.

———

MAHATMA GANDHI

Lifelong learning fuels our soul, boosts our confidence and self-esteem, and can deeply enhance every part of our life. It is what keeps our energy high, our minds active, our inspiration thriving and our opportunities flowing. Albert Einstein famously said, 'Once you stop learning, you start dying', and how right he was. Learning is ongoing, it is voluntary, it requires self-motivation and it is the vehicle for unlocking our true potential.

Learning is the acquisition of knowledge or skills through study, experience or instruction. It is the process of acquiring new or modifying existing knowledge, behaviours, skills, values or preferences. Learning is not simply a task, it is a mindset – a mindset of curiosity that we can adopt by being open, listening more, exploring information and ideas. Many people stop actively learning when they leave the school classroom; however, when we reinstate this growth mindset, we open the door to a new way, we start to flow again, and it can take our life to new heights.

Learning will keep your mind sharp and focused. Like a muscle, it needs daily exercise to stay fit. It will fire your curiosity, give you fresh perspectives on life, upskill you, expose you to new ideas and kickstart your inspiration, both personally and professionally. There has never been a more important time to delve into understanding the world around us and how we can make the most of what is available to us. A grand, soul-nourishing life comes through great learning.

Technology has made being a lifelong student easier than ever before. We don't need to sit in a traditional classroom anymore. We can learn on the move. We can learn through audiobooks, blogs, online courses, podcasts, webinars and so much more. We can research anything at all and deepen our knowledge on any topic of interest, whether it be nutrition, exercise, relationships, investments or specific skills we may need to work on for our career. The challenge is to leave your safe harbour every day, to open up and step out of your comfort zone, to read something different, taste something you've never tried, meet a new person, listen to something unusual and try something you always wanted to.

Think about which topics inspire you and what you want to learn about that will enhance your life. Write down the answer to the three questions on the next page to get you started in each quadrant of life – health, relationships, finance and career.

WHAT DO YOU NEED TO LEARN? – This is to keep you relevant and advancing, healthy and firing.

WHAT DO YOU WANT TO LEARN? – This is to keep you excited, motivated and inspired.

WHAT IS THE BEST WAY TO LEARN IT? – This is so you stay committed, through people, courses, books, listening.

Find something you love and learning will be easy. It will boost your life and make you a more interesting, well-rounded human being.

TOPICS YOU COULD LEARN

How to read faster, how to select good wines, how to cook, how to time-manage, how to write a book, how to take a better photo, how to declutter, how to grow your own vegetables, how to detox your body, how to do yoga, how to use essential oils, how to feng shui your home, how to speak another language, how to play an instrument, how to make bread, how to budget, how to write code and create a web page, how to dance.

SCHEDULE IN LEARNING AS GREAT LEARNERS DO

To keep our curiosity alive, we need to give it some structure so our everyday life doesn't just take over. Learning is a priority; it is the key to growth and it allows us to flourish as it energises our body, mind and soul. Committed learners block out half an hour a day or more to consciously read, listen, write and learn something new about a topic or themselves. They schedule in monthly catch-ups with mentors, they book into courses, conferences, and they network to learn. They have deeper and longer conversations and develop a lust of learning for life. They have a list of topics they are interested in and slowly pursue, making them more interesting people with a depth of character, resulting in more friendships, connections and energy in life. They belong to book clubs and understand that it is a priority above television, gaming and other unrewarding activities.

Learning and success are intertwined. Our capacity to earn is directly related to our willingness to learn. In order to restore yourself, get your flow back and increase your energy, start with a topic you are passionate about, or that simply interests you, and open the door to learning, forever.

19

REINSTATE
BOUNDARIES

Daring to set boundaries is about having the courage to love ourselves even when we risk disappointing others.

———

BRENÉ BROWN

The art of setting boundaries is a life-transforming habit that you can master on a daily basis to reinstate balance in your life. Boundaries are set to protect you from outside influences that rob you of energy, time, health, confidence, happiness and joy. They are the fences that protect, nurture and nourish your most valuable asset: you. They ensure you are living life with purpose, care and a healthy dose of self-respect.

Boundaries need to be strong enough to protect us and yet flexible enough to grow with life, allowing new opportunities and creativity in. Being able to set boundaries is a great indicator of your self-esteem and confidence, and it is a vital skill when you are feeling exhausted and overwhelmed. Boundaries are our quick fix when we need to restore ourselves and reset the goal posts to move forward.

Simple, clearly defined limits for our life give us a road map to make decisions that support and work for us. Boundaries, or personal fences, fuel our health and wellbeing, simplify life and give us space. They keep the 'disease to please' in check, protect our energy stores and keep us connected to our true and authentic selves. They help us to be aware of our own thoughts and feelings and not focus on the thoughts of others. In this space we move to the rhythm that keeps us motivated and inspired.

By setting effective boundaries, we don't tend to take on other people's problems and we are able to prioritise our own health and wellbeing. We learn to communicate clearly and concisely with calm confidence, and we often become role models for others in the process. The result of establishing these protective, workable and reasonable guidelines for ourselves is living the life we want to live with more energy, empathy, warmth, joy, clarity, vision and kindness. The most favourable outcome is that we keep anger and resentment at bay as we feel more in control of our situations and circumstances.

Not setting boundaries can result in resentment, financial burden, stress, anger, career dissatisfaction, wasted time, relationship issues and poor health. There are negative impacts in all areas of life that can fully deplete us physically, mentally and emotionally if we don't put boundaries in place.

TOP TIPS TO REINSTATE BALANCE WITH BOUNDARIES

Identify your core values and use them as a guide for what is most important in life. For example, if health is a priority, set boundaries around your diet, sleep and exercise.

Set up and communicate some of the basic boundaries with friends and family. Communicate what you are doing so others have the opportunity to support you rather than tempt you to go off course.

Get clarity on what is non-negotiable and what is flexible – bedtime is 10 pm unless there is a function, party or emergency.

Establish your most comfortable and gracious way of saying 'no'. Have two to three ways to protect yourself from the desire to please. 'Thanks for the invitation but unfortunately I am already committed. I look forward to the next opportunity.'

Decide how to deal with consequences ahead of time. Think through the scenarios and what your responses may be.

Develop a healthy respect for yourself. Your own sense of self and respect for what is important will safeguard you from others who want to define or control you. You are the guard.

Be in charge of your choices. Make sure they support, nourish and nurture you.

Remember it is not your job to make someone else happy. Happiness comes from the inside.

Many people feel guilty, scared and uncomfortable getting in the driver's seat and taking control by setting boundaries, but they are the backbone of a healthy life with respectful relationships and self-care. They don't need to be suffocating, they should be viewed more as liberating. They celebrate who you are and what you value, stand for and believe in.

BOUNDARIES FOR INSTANT RENEWAL

FOOD – No coffee after 2 pm, smaller portions, cut out refined sugar, no alcohol during the week.

SLEEP – Up at 6 am, bed by 10 pm, journal before bed.

EXERCISE – Set clothes out the night before, exercise daily. Our favourite saying is, 'Tomorrow starts today.'

TECHNOLOGY – Set a technology blackout period 9 pm–7 am. No screens in bedrooms. Use an alarm clock.

SPENDING – Set yourself a budget challenge, don't shop at sales when you don't need anything. Before buying, ask yourself, 'Do I need it? Do I want it? Will I treasure it?'

TIME WITH FRIENDS – Organise a get-together twice a month, let friends know what time you need to leave at the start of the catch-up or phone call.

PEOPLE TO ESTABLISH BOUNDARIES WITH

- Significant other
- Family members
- Co-workers
- Boss
- Room-mate
- Friends

Healthy boundaries will restore your energy and bring you back to your authentic and wonderful self. They will guide you, protect you, enrich your life, relationships and health and define you. They will help you to be more organised, give you some accountability, let you love yourself for who you are, change your habits to support you, boost your confidence and bring you back to your heart centre.

Develop a daily boundary-setting practice. It is the solution to work–life balance.

20

restore

REFINE YOUR
PURPOSE

It's the repetition
of affirmations
that leads to belief.
And once that
belief becomes
a deep conviction,
things begin
to happen.

———

MUHAMMAD ALI

To live with purpose each day gives you vitality and fulfilment. It enables you to live a life you are proud of, with joy and inspiration, depth and connection. Personal wellbeing and enrichment lie at the foundation of every success we have in our lives. The rewards are great opportunities and happiness.

Many people spend years searching for their purpose, often robbing themselves of their own happiness if the answer is not easy. Giving ourselves permission to live with a daily purpose sets us up for success, allowing us to celebrate what we have achieved.

The most important part of living with purpose and fulfilment each day is establishing positive routines and rituals that allow you to thrive and fuel your confidence. Dedicating a small amount of time when you first wake, and before you go to bed, can set you up for a great day. It helps us protect and honour who we are, and lets us experience gratitude, kindness and inspiration daily.

Here are some ideas that you can choose from to design your own bookends for the day and use to ground yourself. The most popular and common way to enhance this process is to have a little notebook next to your bed. It is your 'go-to' as you wake and as you prepare for sleep, your anchor point before you set sail in the morning, and what secures you at night.

MORNING ROUTINE

Early to bed, early to rise. When we wake up, we get an incredible opportunity to set up a new day. By having a simple routine, our brains are given the road map for the day. We can program what we want to focus on to drown out some of the distraction, and we get the opportunity to be the driver rather than the passenger – to design our day and not live in default mode, guarding our energy and emotions. There is something incredibly special about being awake early. It is often when the best work of the day is done, and that work is to be done on the business of you.

Establish your routine and make it your new normal. Be consistent. Here are some tips to inspire you to get up and own the first hour of your day. See what works for you. There is no doubt that a powerful morning routine can turn your life around.

> **GET UP EARLIER**   Find a time that suits you so the first hour of the day can be sacred to you.

> **TAKE THREE DEEP BREATHS** before you get out of bed to find joy from your slumber and wake yourself up.

SET YOUR INTENTION FOR THE DAY BEFORE YOU RISE
– To go hard, to just flow, to surrender, to learn, to commit.

WRITE DOWN THREE THINGS YOU ARE GRATEFUL FOR
– Your bed, hot water, friends in your life, the book you just read, your health.

MAKE YOUR BED – It's your first accomplishment and sets the tone for the day.

WRITE IN YOUR JOURNAL – Unpack your mind; you don't know what you really think until you write it down; clarity is the DNA of success and growth.

WRITE DOWN OR CONFIRM YOUR AFFIRMATION OF THE DAY – Directing your mind towards what it needs to focus on. This is your mantra for the day.

CONFIRM WHAT YOU CAN DO TO MAKE TODAY GREAT – Write down the one commitment you will make.

EXERCISE – Walk, run, go to the gym, do yoga, do Pilates, swim, stretch to kickstart your day and metabolism.

FINISH YOUR SHOWER WITH A BLAST OF COLD WATER – This shakes up your system and gets you fired up for the day.

SMILE IN THE MIRROR – Say good morning to yourself.

ESTABLISH A GROUNDING ACTIVITY – Meditation, breathing, reflecting.

TOUCH YOUR GOALS – Set your priority list for the day.

LEARN SOMETHING – Read a few pages of a book, listen to an audiobook or podcast.

DRINK WATER – Your body is thirsty. Try adding lemon and a spoonful of apple cider vinegar.

NIGHT-TIME ROUTINE

It's equally as important to get back to yourself and end the day with control. The following are some rituals that soothe and allow you to reflect on the day. It is in the acknowledgement that we find the lessons and then the peace.

- Evaluate your day.
- Accept today for what it was, make peace with it and let it go.
- Write your to-do list for tomorrow – make a list of priorities, including work and friendship. You can also write down what you do not want to do (for example, no soft drinks) to remind yourself that this is your commitment.
- Set your alarm for the morning.
- Organise your exercise for the morning – plan to meet a buddy, book a class, set up your yoga mat.
- Disconnect – turn off technology an hour before your bedtime to settle the mind.
- Read to wind down – even one chapter of a book, or something you want to learn and improve on that is not work.
- Organise what you will eat for the following day to avoid making compromised choices.

- ∅ Set out your clothes for tomorrow.
- ∅ Write down three amazing things that happened during the day and three things you are grateful for.
- ∅ Write down what would make tomorrow great.
- ∅ Meditate.
- ∅ Go to sleep knowing you have a cracking morning routine that will kickstart your day tomorrow.

The journal is the most powerful tool. Journalling and writing down your thoughts, intentions and feelings, along with keeping a daily gratitude journal, lead to better sleep, reduction in physical pain, a greater sense of wellbeing and a better ability to handle change.

Define your purpose, one day at a time, and become more and more grounded. This is your life and no one else's. Design a rhythm and ritual that sets your soul on fire, that lets you rise up and get stuck into life. You need to accept that it's okay for the journey to be a bit messy and not let perfectionism get in the way of progress. Just start. Just do. Just pick up the pen. Just move. Just take control. This is your time.

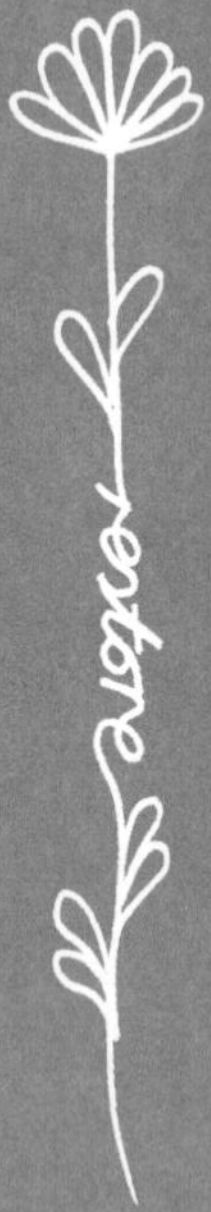
restore

AND
FINALLY

Give yourself time. Be more loving towards yourself. No one knows all the answers. Stop worrying and start living. Delve into your depths; live with love, honesty and trust; nourish your soul; celebrate who you are; and, most importantly, look after yourself. Just start. Just start doing something new, something to honour yourself. You might not end up liking it, but at least then you'll know. You might try one of these skills and it will transform your life!

Restoring yourself will bring you closer to happiness, fulfilment and wholehearted mental, physical, emotional and spiritual health. You will keep changing. Your world will keep changing, but may the connection to yourself never be lost on this great journey called life.

Shannah and Lyndall – The Essentialists

ABOUT THE ESSENTIALISTS

OUR MISSION

The Essentialists work to engage, educate and empower individuals, teams and organisations with essential life and wellness skills.

The Essentialists help people take control of their health, wellbeing, and ultimately their happiness by committing to what is essential in both their personal and professional life, through the mastery of fundamental life and wellness skills. Their commitment is to equip people with the tools they need to make the best, wisest and most authentic investment of their time and energy in their one and only precious life.

The Essentialists' way isn't about doing more, it's about doing what's right for you, wherever you are, in life's journey. This clarity allows for far more effective work and self-care practices that ultimately lead to breakthroughs in work and life. Better leadership, human connections, gratitude, empathy and joy in the everyday. The results of The Essentialists' programs are a testimony to this.

WHO ARE THE ESSENTIALISTS?

Shannah Kennedy and Lyndall Mitchell
Educators of Life and Wellness Skills

Shannah and Lyndall are acknowledged as Australia's leaders in life and wellness education. They combine more than three decades of teaching, presenting and executive coaching experience across public and corporate sectors globally. Their books, *Chaos to Calm: Take Control with Confidence* and *Shine: 20 Secrets to a Happy Life* have helped many people create extraordinary lives.

Together, Shannah and Lyndall offer a wealth of experience, complementary expertise and strategies to maximise impact for their clients. As working mothers juggling family with thriving businesses and a non-negotiable stance on the importance of their own health and wellbeing, their commitment to basic fundamental life skills ensures they stay on track and constantly evolve to be their best.

For speaking opportunities enquire at
info@theessentialists.com.au
Stay inspired, stay connected. Join our global
online community for regular bite sized life
and wellness skills:
theessentialists.com.au
@theessentialistshub

The Essentialists are teaching the most valuable
tools and principles the human spirit needs
in today's world.

KARINA STEWART – KAMALAYA CO-FOUNDER

The Essentialists are committed to teaching the
vital skills to restore, reconnect and nourish
the soul, body and mind.

AGAPI STASSINOPOULOS – AUTHOR

The Essentialists offer simple, practical and
encouraging words of advice to inspire you to
reclaim your energy and empower you once again.

REBECCA HARD – GM SUSSAN

The Essentialists provide an insightful
resource to refuel your tank.

COLLEEN CALLANDER – CEO SPORTSGIRL

ACKNOWLEDGEMENTS

We express our deep appreciation to the entire team at Penguin Random House, who support and believe in our passion to educate the world with essential life and wellness skills.

To our readers and clients who constantly fuel our fire and show gratitude for this incredibly important educational and inspirational work – you keep us fully committed to doing what is essential for us to thrive and live our best lives.